TIME FOR A FEW EXTRA ITEMS

Ian Davidson is the Two Ronnies' Script Associate and the only known person to have written for TW3, appeared on Monty Python and picked their nose on Not the Nine O'Clock News.
He takes bribes.

Other Two Ronnies books in Star

BUT FIRST THE NEWS
NICE TO BE WITH YOU AGAIN
IN A PACKED PROGRAMME TONIGHT
AND IT'S HELLO FROM HIM
THE BUMPER BOOK OF THE TWO RONNIES
THE TWO RONNIES' SKETCHBOOK
RONNIE IN THE CHAIR

TIME FOR A FEW EXTRA ITEMS

Edited by

Ian Davidson

Illustrations by
Ian Heath

A STAR BOOK
published by
the Paperback Division of
W. H. ALLEN & Co. Ltd

A Star Book
Published in 1981
by the Paperback Division of
W. H. Allen & Co. Ltd
A Howard and Wyndham Company
44 Hill Street, London W1X 8LB

Typeset by Computacomp (UK) Ltd,
Fort William, Scotland

Printed in Great Britain by
Hunt Barnard Printing Ltd., Aylesbury, Bucks.

ISBN 0 352 30958 X

Comedy writers wear corduroy jackets and Hush Puppies, avoid barbers, constantly lose their pencils and cut themselves shaving. And that's only the women. The following are extremely talented.

Peter Bain, Howard Baker, Alec Baron, John Bilsborough, Ray Binns, Norman Braidwood, George Brodie & Mike Perry, Alex Brown & Pat Murray, Colin Brown, Phil Campbell, Jonathan Canter, Simon Cheshire, Niall Clark, John Cotterill, Bernard Cranwell, Phil David, Dave Dutton, Alan Edwards, Pete Edwards, Paul Eldergill, Barry Faulkner, Ernest Forbes, Fuzz, Phil Gould, John Griffin, Bob Groocock, Neville Gurnhill, Stephen Hancocks, Les Higgins, Tim Hopkins, Bob Hedley, P. J. Kaye, David Kind, Michael Knowles, Geoff Leack, Roland Lester, Ed McHenry, Wally McKinley, Tom Magee Englefield, Gerald Mahlowe, George Martin, Ron Missellbrook, Phil Munnoch, Gavin Osbon, Cy Parry, Ray Price, Mike Radford, Robert Randall, Terry Ravenscroft, Glyn Rees, Tony Rich, Peter Robinson, Laurie Rowley, Tony Stevens, Robert Sykes Andrews, Laurie Teague, Terry Treloar, Peter Vincent, David Webb, Tony Wheatley, Alan Wightman, Tony Wyatt, Keith Valentine.

Editor's Note: Keep up the good work, lads.

Here they come, Corber and Barklett, sprucely jacketed as newscasters ready to start another show rolling ... Little do the audience at home know that they're wearing guardsmen's trousers and ammunition boots ready for the first sketch. The studio audience got their first private laugh ... Now come the big laughs that start and finish the show—and here they all are, plus some that never reached the screen, in a packed paperback tonight. ...

GOOD EVENING

Ronnie Corbett: It's wonderful to be back with you once again, isn't it, Ronnie?

Ronnie Barker: Indeed it is. And in a packed programme tonight ...
We'll be talking to a man who played truant from correspondence college by sending back empty envelopes.

RC: And I'll be talking to the Birmingham man who met his wife at a Fancy Dress Party. She went as a pile of pennies and he took her outside and found she was a pushover.

RB: Then we'll be having a word with Tiddles the cat who never gets lost and we'll be learning the secret of his success. He only eats homing pigeons.

RC: But, first, the news. It was announced today that Percy Edwards and twenty-five farmyard impressionist friends are getting together to do an LP of the House of Commons.

RB: A British cosmetic company has produced a new deodorant called 'Unseen'. It doesn't work but it makes you invisible.

RC: Scientists at London Zoo have finally discovered why the two Giant Pandas have failed to mate. The parrot in the next cage works for Mrs. Whitehouse.

RB: J. Thimble-Glutt, the Middlesborough man who doesn't smoke, drink or gamble and has never had a girlfriend, tried to celebrate his fortieth birthday today, but couldn't think how.

GOBBLE!
GRUNT! GOBBLE!
MOOOOO!
COCK-A-DOODLE-DOO!
BAA! BAA! NEIGH!
CLUCK! CLUCK!
QUACK!
SAY BUDDY, IS THIS LONDON ZOO?
BOUTIQUE

RC: Engineers from the BBC and ITV have designed a revolutionary new video recorder. While you're out it tapes all the programmes you hate and then plays them all back while you're on holiday.

RB: Whilst at London's Heathrow, senior Customs Officer Cephas Mumby, retired today. So he confiscated a gold watch for himself.

RC: Also news tonight that Mr. Norman St. John Stevas has at last been able to arrange an audience with the Pope. Up until now, Norman hadn't been able to spare the time.

... But now a sketch in which I play the very important part of Casanova. ...

RB: And I play the rest of him.

ADIDAS JOIN BADIDAS TO MAKE VERY SOFT SHOES

RB: Sport. At the White City tonight, a Russian athlete who cleared 18 feet in the Long Jump was beaten into second place during the interval by a Max Bygraves record which cleared the entire stadium.

RC: Seamus O'Toole's shattering of the world 100 yards record by an amazing six seconds last night in Dublin has not been ratified. The judges say he must have taken a short cut.

RB: And at the Albert Hall tonight, the fight for the World Short Sighted boxing title was stopped in the ninth round to save the referee from further punishment.

RC: Former Olympic horsewoman, Atalanta Pendleton-Mowbray-Hicks began a new career in Soho today. She's opened a dressage parlour.

RB: Police are tonight searching for the Fulham supporter who waited for Jimmy Hill after 'Match of the Day' and threatened to knock the living highlights out of him.

RC: Biffer Kilgariff, Britain's foulest footballer was at a testimonial lunch today given him on his retirement by the Referees Association. They gave him a terrific send-off.

RB: Dutch striker Budget van Rental was badly hurt after scoring a goal this afternoon. Nobody kissed him.

RC: And the Fourth Division's worst goalkeeper, Ernie Clack, failed to sign for a new club today. He kept dropping the pen.

RB: Bulldog Clip, the Stockport County supporter who was so upset by his team's performance that he ran blaspheming onto the pitch, appeared before magistrates today. He was fined £5 and given six months in goal.

RC: And the First Division's stroppiest player, Dingle Preen, was nearly involved in an accident this afternoon when the dressing room caught fire and he refused to move back ten yards.

HARRY ACKROYD, SELF-STYLED STEAK AND KIDNEY PUDDING KING, WAS BURIED TODAY—ALONG WITH HIS SECRET RECIPE. RELATIVES SAID THAT IF THE INGREDIENTS ARE EVER REVEALED HE'LL TURN IN HIS GRAVY.

HERE LYETH HARRY ACKROYD AND HIS SECRET RECIPE
R.I.P.
Ian heath

LATER IN THE PROGRAMME...

RB: We'll be talking to the very generous landlord of the George and Dragon pub who every Sunday picks out a customer down on his luck and gives him the right change.

RC: And in a new religious section of the programme I'll be talking to a nail-biter who gave himself up for Lent.

RB: And we hope we'll be introducing Vernon Wegsby, the nudist who fitted a magnifying glass to his fig leaf and reflected great credit on himself.

RC: But, first, the news. Unemployed storeman Felix Fainites turned up for a job in a furniture store today in his Klu Klux Klan robes. He was immediately taken on as a dust sheet.

RB: Security was tight at Heathrow today. Accounts were merry and the loaders were out of their tiny minds.

RC: A group of Irish people who are sick and tired of Irish jokes set out today to march on London. They were last seen thirty miles outside Grimsby going north.

RB: At today's Conference of the Forgetful Society, the chairman gave the keynote speech. He said 1980 had been a whatnot of whatjamacallits. Whatshername and Whojamaflip had made a complete thingummybob. He then sat down on a doodah and hurt his whatsits.

IRISH JOKES OUT!
NO
NO IRISH JOKES
BAN IRISH JO
NO! IRISH
NO TO IRISH JOKES

RC: British Rail today opened their first booking office cum betting shop. This means you can buy a ticket *and* put a bet on whether or not there'll be a driver for your train.

RB: And a happy outcome for Rear Admiral Sir Percy Hodgkinson after he fell into a vat of fresh whipped cream this morning in Portsmouth. He was piped aboard ship this afternoon.

RC: In the sketch which follows, dealing with the geography of the world, I shall be demonstrating Mercator's Projection.

RB: And I shall be asking him to put it away.

BE UPSTANDING...

RB: In London today, a man who forged a bus pass was ordered to do 100 hours community service, and a man who forged a Cup Final ticket was ordered to do 100 hours community singing.

RC: At the trial of the last of the Great Train robbers today the judge put on a black cap and sentenced him to a season ticket.

RB: Dodsworth Sinclair, the Surrey man accused today of TV licence evasion said that he thought having a photo-copy of last year's would be enough because he only intended to watch repeats.

RC: Bendini, the circus acrobat who claims he can make love on a curtain rail, appeared in court today, charged with attempting to drape three women.

RB: For making improper remarks to Shirley Bassey, Shirley Maclaine and Shirley Williams, a man was fined today and will be privately prosecuted by the ladies tomorrow. He claimed tonight that he was being got by the court and Shirleys.

RC: Disaster struck Vic Spin the Human Top last night when he got into a wobble and demolished the Dog and Duck pub. He was later charged by police with being drunk and disorientated.

RC: The man found lying in a Soho gutter last night wearing a latex wet-suit, wellingtons and a rubber gas mask was today found not guilty of being drunk, but fined twenty pounds for having less than the required depth of tread.

RB: And in court today, garage owner Monty Ripoff pleaded not guilty to turning the clock back on a number of cars at his garage in Chelsea. He stated that at the time of the offence he was 10,000 miles away in Fulham.

Ianheath

RB: Topless bacardi waitress Linda Muchacha was fined today for rumbustious behaviour.

THEN WE'LL BE MEETING...

RC: Then we'll be meeting the young executive who whisked his girlfriend across town in a limousine by American Express, bought her dinner on his Diner's Club card but got nothing in the way of Access.

RB: We'll be talking to a man whose hairpiece makes him look thirty years sillier.

IanHeath

RC: And interviewing the man who's too lazy to take his teeth out at night so now he sleeps in a six foot glass of water.

RB:	But first ... There was a full scale alert of Britain's Armed Forces today, followed by a small scale alert of Britain's Action Men.
RC:	A complete security blanket was provided at Gatwick today for the author of Peanuts. So he sucked it.
RB:	A Fulham couple who met four years ago at a local bus stop had two reasons to celebrate today. First, they got married, and then the bus came along.
RC:	At Radstock tonight, two amorous stick insects rubbed themselves together and set light to the local Boy Scouts' hut.
RB:	At the Hospital for Tropical Diseases today, laboratory staff came out on strike. Doctors came out in sympathy and passers-by came out in spots.
RC:	The Bionic Man was released from hospital tonight after falling in the Thames. Doctors told him to spend a few days at home rusting.
RB:	And Mr. Reginald Chubb, the train driver who criticised his colleagues for inefficiency, has been sent to Coventry. He arrived three hours late.

RC: Finally, the Bishop of Brent Cross at today's Diocesan Hunger Lunch reminded his listeners that Charity begins at home but usually finishes up at somebody else's place.

But now a sketch featuring Mr. Ronnie Barker, holder of the Guinness Book of Records title for getting the least number of people into a telephone kiosk.

THE FUNERAL OF DUSTMAN ARNOLD PURGE TOOK PLACE TODAY AT WARBLETON CEMETERY. LATER, HIS ASHES WERE SCATTERED UP AND DOWN SOMEBODY'S FRONT PATH.

OI!
Ianheath

IF YOU PUT IT IN A SKETCH, NOBODY WOULD BELIEVE IT...

RB: We'll be talking to Cyril Lathbottom, the M.P. who dreamt he was giving a speech in the House of Commons and woke up and found he was.

RC: ... and talking to a little old lady who holds up banks. She can't find her glasses to look for a pen.

RB: Then we'll meet the horsewoman who covered her horse with lettuce and tomato because she wanted to ride side-salad.

RC: ... and the only football hooligan known to be a member of Friends of the Earth. When he throws a bottle at a player he shouts 'Recycle that, then!'

RB: ... and the Irish wife who has never found a hair on her husband's coat and thinks he's having an affair with a bald woman.

RC: ... a man who's in prison for something he didn't do. He didn't wear gloves.

RB: ... meeting a man with a magnetic personality and hearing about his deviation.

RC: And finally, we'll be meeting Betty Buxom, the Soho girl who recently bought herself a speedboat. She'll be telling us what it's like to sell yourself right down the river.

UNFORTUNATELY...

RB: We had hoped to have been bringing you Arthur the Human Chameleon but this afternoon he crawled across a tartan rug and died of exhaustion.

RC: But we will be talking to the Labour M.P. who's been putting turf in his underpants in the hope of getting grass roots support.

RB: And having a word with the secretary who made love to her boss on a Sunday and gave him the time and a half of his life.

RC: But first ... A coach carrying forty stuntmen to a convention in London this afternoon ran out of control on the M1. It crossed the central reservation, bounced off a juggernaut, fell fifty feet down an embankment, turned seven double somersets, burst into flames and blew up. No one was hurt.

RB: Absent minded womaniser Simeon Longbottom admitted today that he had had misgivings but couldn't remember any misdoings and was sure he'd never even met Miss Whatnot.

RC: Egbert Grove, Britain's Worst Train Driver was today disciplined by the Railways Board for taking his train through a red light. At the junction of Tottenham Court Road and Oxford Circus.

RB: The Sheffield woman who's been trying out the new roast beef flavoured Pill announced today that she's got a Yorkshire pudding in the oven.

RC: Ariana Stassinopoulous was surprised by a sex maniac today when he attacked Bernard Levin.

RB: A Government Spokesman said today that Britain will be playing her part in the new NATO defence package. We'll be supplying the brown paper and string.

RC: It's been a bad week for Brandon Truscott, the Steeple Aston man who doesn't know the difference between fixative and laxative. His teeth have been stuck on the lavatory since Sunday.

RB: Finally, we must apologise for a mistake in last week's show. When referring to Olaf Trygvasson, the Norwegian pop star, we should have said 'and Astrid his Danish girl friend' and *not* 'astride his Danish girl friend'.

RC: But now a sketch featuring Mr. Ronnie Barker who was today accused by his mother in law of driving too close to the car behind.

WE HAVE THE TECHNOLOGY

RC: We'll be talking to the car designer who's crossed Toyota with Quasimodo—and come up with the Hatchback of Notre Dame.

RB: We'll also be meeting the disc jockey who crossed a little raver with a contortionist and got a girl who does requests on the back of a postcard.

RC: . . . and a man who crossed a ball point pen with a shark and got a fish that writes threatening letters.

RB: . . . and scientists who crossed an Irishman with a homing pigeon and a parrot and got a bird that keeps landing and asking the way.

RC: Whilst the Thundersley man who crossed a Swiss Cheese plant, a Bread Fruit plant and an India Rubber tree today had his first crop of British Rail sandwiches.

'MORNING! — JUST A POSTCARD FOR YOUR HUSBAND!
G.P.O.
Ian heath

PROVIDED WE CAN PACK EVERYTHING IN...

RB: Later in the programme Lin Chun will be here to show us the lotus position and then James Hunt will show us how much easier it is in the back of a Maserati.

RC: Then I'll be telling you the hard luck story of the Exeter woman who advertised for a sugar daddy and only got replies from lollipop men.

WOULD YOU GO BEHIND THE SCREEN AND TAKE OFF YOUR LEAVES!
Ian heath

RB: And an NHS tree surgeon will be telling us he's planning to take on privet patients.

RC: But first ... F. C. Rawles, the Redcar man who has faithfully handed his wife his wage packet every month for the last twenty years, was divorced today. She found out he was paid every week.

RB: British Rail officials helped to clear up after a mishap at Euston Station today, when a container of spices broke open. The South East Divisional Manager shovelled cloves and Peter Parker picked a peck of pickled peppers.

RC: And there was surprising news today for Sandra Micklethwaite, the Nottingham woman who recently made love on the Big Wheel. She's in the Rotary Club.

RB: The Irish TUC decided today that tomorrow's ballot will be secret. There will be a show of hands but everybody will be blindfolded.

RC: And at a special meeting of the executive committee of the Extremely Shy and Painfully Self-Conscious Society tonight the members gave themselves a vote of no confidence.

RB: Fishermen in the Firth of Clyde have caught three nuclear submarines in their nets this year and as a result have received a stern warning. Two more and they've reached their quota.

RC: And, finally, Epraim Sludge, who has worked in sewers all his life, was today knighted by the Queen, using a ten foot barge pole.

RB: But now a sketch in which Mr. Ronnie Corbett will be showing how he uses cotton wool buds for all his important little places. He'll be cleaning out his Wendy House.

ARISE SIR EPRAIM!
Ianheath

PUT THIS STOCKING OVER YOUR HEAD AND DO GET THE SEAM STRAIGHT FOR ONCE

RB: We've just heard that following the riot at Dublin Prison, the Governor has decided to call in the bailiffs and evict the troublemakers.

RC: Super-grass Pidgin O'Stool yesterday told how his only ambition is to become a pillar of the Church. Several of his oldest friends were out today buying sand and cement.

RB: This afternoon thieves broke into the luxury home of Rasmus Backstop, the budgerigar cage millionaire. He claims they totally cleaned him out.

RC: And it was good news today for the Edgbaston man gaoled for five years for stealing records. He's being re-released on Friday.

RB: Thieves broke into the BBC's make up Department here at Shepherds Bush last night and escaped with cuts and bruises.

THE CREMATION TOOK PLACE TODAY OF TONY EASTGATE, THE CHAIRMAN OF THE WICKFORD DISTRICT HIGHWAYS COMMITTEE. TO COMMEMORATE A LIFE SPENT IN THE PUBLIC SERVICE, HIS ASHES WERE SCATTERED ON A PARTICULARLY NASTY PATCH OF ICE IN THE ROAD OUTSIDE.

HERE IN THE STUDIO...

RB: We'll be showing you a new and reliable method for contacting the dead—just dial 100 and wait.

RC: We'll be talking to a well-equipped specialist plumber who goes out on jobs armed with everything bar the kitchen sink. He's a kitchen sink installer.

RB: And I'll be interviewing the Sussex lady who switched on her old hedge cutter this afternoon and had a lot of trouble calming him down.

RC: But first . . . the economy. Tomorrow the Government will introduce tough new measures. They are expected to include the butch foot, the macho metre and the bull dyke mile.

RB: The BMA today gave Dr. Erasmus Honeydew its highest award in token of its high regard for his work in persuading people not to smoke. Dr. Honeydew is the inventor of the cigarette vending machine which doesn't work.

RC: Merryweather Tilsden, who's a hundred years old next week, said today that he plans to celebrate the occasion by making love. The Queen is sending him a telegram and the Duke of Edinburgh is sending him a diagram.

100 TODAY

RB: Mary Whitehouse took time off from her Radio One phone-in programme today to go for a breather in the park. His condition tonight is said to be 'comfortable'.

RC: The Soho Girls' pay negotiations took a new turn today with the girls demanding more money on the table, a lot more money on the floor and danger money on the chandelier.

RB: Explorers on a remote Pacific island have discovered a Japanese soldier who didn't know the war was over, an Irishman who didn't know it had even begun, and a drunken Scotsman who wanted to start it again.

RC: Published today were the results of last month's referendum on drinking. 20% put Yes please; 11% put No thank you; and the other 69% put the ballot box to their lips and blew.

RB: Finally, Royston Kildare, the Dewsbury man who wants various parts of his body to be used in transplant operations was out practising this morning. He offered his seat to a woman on a bus.

... but now a sketch featuring Mr. Ronnie Corbett—a self-made man who ran short of material.

PROCEEDING IN AN EVER-DECREASING CIRCULAR DIRECTION...

RB: The big roll of Sellotape left behind by the Bond Street safe-breakers remains a mystery. Police are working on the theory that it's a glue-sniffer's packed lunch.

RC: A staggering bleary-eyed man ran away today after shouting obscenities at a bus conductor and refusing to pay his fare. Police suspect eight million Scotsmen.

RB: The handicrafts teacher from Bolton who was arrested six months ago is still in police custody. She's believed to be embroidering her alibi.

RC: Latest on the bullion robbery. At Wandsworth police station, a man who's as deaf as a post, and doesn't speak English, with a terrible stutter, bad breath and squeaky shoes, is not helping police with their inquiries one little bit.

RB: The Metropolitan Police today denied that prisoners in their custody are excessively pampered. This follows yesterday's report that a man was hustled out of New Scotland Yard with an electric blanket over his head.

RC: Devon police raided a black magic ceremony on Dartmoor last night and took away all the Hazelnut Clusters.

RB: Tooting Bec police today arrested a man in connection with a thirteen amp plug and blacked out most of South London.

RC: Whilst, in West Mercia, police announced tonight that they wished to interview a man wearing high heels and frilly knickers. But the Chief Constable says they must wear their uniforms.

SPOILSPORT!
Ianheath

RB: A holdup at the wages office of a timber yard was foiled today by a workman with a chain-saw. Police are looking for a sawn-off man with a shotgun.

RC: The frail 67-year-old lady who walked out of Harrods carrying four new night storage heaters she hadn't paid for told police tonight that she did it in a moment of weakness.

WEARING OUR THRUSTING PROBING HATS...

RB: We'll be investigating allegations of slow service in the Post Office and finding out why the Queen now has to send telegrams to people who are only ninety-seven.

RC: And, in our new Natural History feature, we'll be having a look at amazing wildlife footage of Italian birds surrendering to a worm.

RB: And then we'll be going over to see Dolly Parton packing them in at the Gamages Corset Department.

RC: But first . . . Second prize in the British Airways contest to find their Most Travelled Passenger has gone to Mr. Burslem Throttleby, who's flown 70,000 miles in the last six months. First prize went to his luggage which has done 90,000.

2
1

RB: Roland Perks, the Islington man whose wife had a ten year affair with a home improvement contractor said today 'I had no reason to suspect them'. Mr. Perks was speaking from his twelve-bedroomed, three-bathroomed, double-garaged, solar heated en suite prefab.

RC: A fire has completely destroyed the Wonderland miniature village in Torquay. At the height of the blaze, the flames could be seen almost three feet away.

RB: The cold weather which is afflicting New York continues. The city's most notorious flasher, Ferdinando Gonzales, now jumps out and describes himself.

RC: Ginger, the first cat ever to go into space, had a nasty experience today. He was seen to by the Flying Doctor.

RB: And we've just heard that a juggernaut of onions has shed its load all over the M1. Motorists are advised to find a hard shoulder to cry on.

RC: The condition of the man who thinks he's an 'O' Level has improved. Now he's dressed up as the Three Degrees.

PSYCHIATRIST
YOU'RE O.K! —YOU JUST CAN'T SING!

. . . and now a sketch featuring Mr. Ronnie Barker whose family theatrical tradition started when his grandfather went to America and got stage-struck. He was run over by Wells Fargo.

NEWS OF SUPER STARS, INCLUDING SOME YOU'VE NEVER HEARD OF...

RB: At a press conference today, excited movie executives announced that Julie Andrews will appear topless in her next movie, to be released next year and provisionally titled 'Mary Poppouts'.

RC: The Department of Fair Trading has been called in to investigate the latest SingalongaMax concert after complaints that Max Bygraves got paid nine thousand pounds and the audience did most of the singing.

RB: Britain's top punk star, Des Dirty, whose personal habits have outraged millions, caused another sensation tonight when he announced his intention to go on the road.

RC: The rabbit epic 'Watership Down' is being released again. The story is the same but now it has a cast of thousands.

RB: Tonight saw the opening in the West End of Paul Raymond's new full-frontal Agatha Christie thriller. When asked who did it, firstnighters replied 'Everybody'.

RC: Quick change artist Prestini came a cropper last night when, after changing into Mae West, Robin Day and Basil Brush in quick succession, he turned into a one-way street on his way home and was resurfaced by the Council.

RB: American singing star Dolly Parton was tonight reported to have found the favourite guitar she lost twenty years ago. It was up her jumper.

RC: Five hundred people had a miraculous escape at a Charles Aznavour concert tonight. He didn't turn up.

RB: So there we are. Later in the programme I'll be talking to struggling young actress Virginia Cherry straight from a disappointing casting session in the West End. She'll say she wants to give up the stage and I'll advise her to give up struggling.

RC: But now a sketch set on the Costa Smeralda, the Aga Khan's private resort which is so exclusive that yesterday the tide went out and they wouldn't let it back in.

THE BURIAL TOOK PLACE TODAY OF PORN-PUBLISHER LAFCADIO TWILL. AS THE PLAIN BROWN WRAPPER WAS LOWERED INTO THE GROUND, A LARGE CROWD OF MOURNING READERS PRETENDED THEY WERE LOOKING AT ANOTHER FUNERAL.

WE'LL BE HEARING...

RB: ... about the chicken that laid a 28 pound egg and is now suffering from shellshock.

RC: And we'll be meeting the man who only three months ago went into business making miniaturised pocket calculators. And things are already going so well that he's looking for smaller premises.

DESIRABLE
BUSINESS PREMISES
FOR SALE
APPLY
I'LL TAKE IT!

RB: The West London transplant patient who recently received the heart of a dog and the kidneys of a rabbit made history tonight when he chased himself three times round White City dog track and won.

RC: Stretcho, the rubber band man, has been sacked from Lord George Davidson's circus because he got on everyone's nerves, sitting around twanging himself.

RB: In the little-known African state of Umpopoland, doctors have appealed for help after running out of leeches. Britain is to airlift in two hundred estate agents.

RC: Sad news of the Tadcaster man who failed to keep up the hire purchase payments on his exorcism and was today repossessed.

RB: Britain's strangest ever wedding took place in London today when a man who used to be a woman married a woman who used to be a man. The bride's mother used to be a male nurse, the best man used to be the bridesmaid and the wedding cake started life as a french tart.

RC: The long awaited Government report on illiteracy will be published next month, just as soon as they've finished dotting the b's and crossing the w's.

RB: The Meteorological Office's Long Range Forecast today predicted a mild winter next year. Instead of a summer.

RC: The President of the French Garlic Growers coughed loudly in Paris today and gave the kiss of life to a man in Torquay.

RB: And now a sketch starring Mr. Ronnie Corbett, in which I gave him Sonia Lannaman's phone number and he tries to pull a fast one.

SPONSORSHIP LATEST: BRITISH 100 METRE MEN TO GET A PENNY A MILE

RC: Show jumper Jane Smyth failed her driving test today when her car knocked over a five-barred gate, cut things close at the water and finally refused at the seven foot wall.

L
FA IL

RB: Archie Drax, Britain's slowest sprinter, proved his critics wrong at Crystal Palace tonight. He caught a cold.

RC: And during re-decoration at Brentford Public Library today high jumper Farrington Bland accidentally sat on a blowlamp and leapt straight into the record books.

RB: Albert Baggs, Fulham's leading supporter, began a new job as a chef today. To make him feel at home he was relegated to the washing-up.

RC: In the British Rail Tennis Championships this week, a Surrey engine driver was forced to retire from the Mixed Doubles after a low ball in the midland region left his services severely disrupted.

RB: And in tonight's Three A's High Jump finals at Wembley, Graham Tonge of Basildon didn't jump high enough, hit the bar and was eliminated. Tom Bassett jumped too high, hit an overhead cable and was illuminated.

RC: The New Zealand Rugby touring team's match against an All-Gay Fifteen ended tonight in a nil–nil draw, even though the Gays had eight tries and a conversion.

RB: Ron Greenwood has announced that the England side for this week's international remains unchanged. Kevin Keegan will wear the same shirt, Dave Watson will wear his usual shorts and Trevor Brooking will dominate the mid-field in a pair of socks that would knock the top of your head off.

RC: And, finally, it was a bad day for the monkey at Whipsnade's Animal Olympics. He was so upset at only being runner-up in the pole vault, he put the shot where he usually puts his nuts.

OUR OUTSIDE BROADCAST CAMERAS WILL BE AT...

RB: . . . Brighton Station to see delegates gathering for this weekend's conferences—Taxidermists, Nudists and Gay Train Spotters. The booking hall will be full of stuff buffs, buff buffs and puff puff buff puffs.

RC: And we'll be talking to radio personalities who've taken up self defence. There'll be a disc jockey who's a green belt in ju-jitsu, a newsreader who's a black belt in judo and an actor who's a Fifth Dan in the Archers.

RB: But first . . . the Norman Ferzackerley Pornographic Choir will be here to sing 'A way in a Manger' and 'Another Way in a Haystack'.

RC: 'Which?' reports today that the most effective scarecrow on the market is the new Margaret Thatcher look-alike. Not only do the birds not eat the seeds, they bring back the ones they took last year.

RB: An Oxford University professor has returned from the Middle East with the Dead Sea Scrolls. However it's clearing up nicely and he'll be back at work on Monday.

RC: Rough House Row, Tower Hamlets, which is London's toughest street, held a party today for its oldest inhabitant. He'll be twenty-three on Monday.

RB: On sale in Moscow today; perfectly-preserved frozen steaks of Siberian mammoth from the last Ice Age. A spokesman said they are cheap and nutritious but take one hundred thousand years to defrost.

RC: Finally, the strong winds which swept southern England last night caused extensive damage to the Royal Mint. They also made a mess of the Royal Rhubarb.

RB: But good news tonight from Hunslet Cottage Hospital—the man who ate Brillo pads in mistake for Shredded Wheat is expected to scrape through.

... but now a sketch featuring Mr. Ronnie Corbett, a man who freely admits that sex manuals have improved his love life. He stands on them.

SOMETHING OUGHT TO BE DONE TO STOP THESE EXPERIMENTS...

RC: We'll be talking to the man who crossed a Rhode Island Red with a ouija board and got a chicken that gets in touch with the other side of the road.

RB: ... then with the disappointed Egyptologist who crossed Nefertiti with Titicaca and got two sets of Nefercaca's.

RC: ... and to the farmer who crossed a gossip columnist with an apple and got a Golden Malicious.

RB: ... to the Dewsbury man who crossed a raver with the Noise Abatement Society and got a bit on the quiet.

RC: . . . and a man who crossed a padded bra with Plaster of Paris and got a completely false impression.

RB: But, meanwhile, scientists in California have crossed a migraine and a migrant and come up with a headache that flies south for the winter.

PERCIVAL DOODAH, THE NINETY-FIVE-YEAR-OLD HYPOCHONDRIAC WHO TREATED ALL HIS OWN AILMENTS FROM A MEDICAL ENCYCLOPAEDIA, DIED TODAY OF A MISPRINT..

I'LL SUE THAT DAMN PUBLISHER!
lanheath

WE WILL BE GAINING AN INSIGHT INTO...

RC: ... the man who goes in for meditation because he thinks it's better than sitting around doing nothing.

RB: And we'll be meeting the crime writer whose new novel has a surprise ending—the murderer is somebody from another book.

RC: We'll be talking to the Dalek who got the sack today when they found him in his dressing room making love to the waste paper bin.

RB: But first . . . Half the workforce at a club in Manchester walked out tonight in a dispute over manning. The other half stayed behind to see if the rest of his jokes were any better.

RC: Irish Leyland have announced that this year should be a bumper year. Next year will be a radiator year and you should have the whole car by 1993.

RB: Whilst at Swizzlewick, Yorks, this afternoon, the lady Mayoress unveiled a large bust outside the Town Hall when she caught her blouse in the car door handle.

RC: Mr. Wally Turnham has again won the Most Amorous Milkman of the Year Award. Apparently he's so popular with his lady customers that he's started to leave notes on their doorsteps saying 'None today thank you'.

RB: British Rail announced plans today for multilingual announcements at Waterloo Station. Now nobody in the whole world will be able to understand them.

AT LEAST HE'S GOING IN THE RIGHT DIRECTION!
Ian heath

ALFRED HONEYBALL, INVENTOR OF THE REVOLUTIONARY HONEYBALL GUNPOWDER DIET WAS LAID TO REST TODAY.
HE LEAVES A WIFE, A DAUGHTER, AND A BIG HOLE WHERE THE CREMATORIUM USED TO BE.

RC: The President of the Society of People who like Eating Rotten Food said today that their annual picnic had been a tremendous success with everything going off really well.

RB: Victor Tinney, East Midlands North's Worst Plumber was sent home again today with hot flushes.

RC: And now a sketch in which Mr. Ronnie Barker plays the part of Gabriele d'Annunzio, reformed Italian gangster turned chef, who is haunted by his pasta.

THATS JUST ABOUT ALL

RB: ... we seem to have space for in this book, isn't it, Ron?

RC: Indeed it is. But before we finish, here's a few late items of news.

Reports that the Royal Navy is extremely badly equipped were denied by the First Sea Lord today when he launched the Fleet's newest courgette.

RB: A man was to have been arraigned by the grand jury of Socatoomee, Wis., today on a charge of 180 degree murder but he'd shot himself.

RC: And there was bad news this morning for relatives, neighbours and friends at the reading of the will of J. Septimus Cadge, Britain's worst borrower. He left everything he owed to charity.

RB: Trainee skin divers Bob and Betty Bletchley set a new record today after asking their instructor if it was possible to have sex in six feet of water and being told to fathom it out for themselves.

RC: Mr. Cyril Smith confounded critics of his appearance today by revealing that his suits are made in Savile Row—and the two adjoining streets.

RB: At Fulham Registry Office today the manager of a do-it-yourself shop married the manageress of a self service canteen. They had their first quarrel half an hour later when both of them refused to cut the cake.

RC: Finally, Arnold Plunger, Britain's oldest plumber was today called to meet his Maker. He said he'd be round in about three weeks.

RB: Next year we'll be hearing of the impact of silicone treatments in Nurseryland when we talk to Not-So-Little Bo-Peep, Far-From-Little Miss Muffett and Enormous Jack Horner.

RC: And seeing a demonstration of a new lager for easy-going girls which claims to refresh the parts that anyone can reach.

RB: And we'll be revealing what Civil Servants have for lunch—about four and a half hours.

RC: Until then, it's goodbye from me.

RB: And goodbye from him.

THAT'LL BE SEVENTY-SIX PENCE, PLEASE!
TAP ROOM